Michael Rose

Devil May Care

Clink
Street

Published by Clink Street Publishing 2023

Copyright © 2023

First edition.

The author asserts the moral right under the Copyright, Designs and Patents Act 1988 to be identified as the author of this work.

ISBN:
978-1-915785-17-6 - paperback
978-1-915785-18-3 - ebook

FORBIDDEN FRUIT

don't think for one moment it was
a boring old apple
the piece of fruit they traded paradise for
was a waitrose speciality rich and jammy fig

dark purple dusted with a haze of bloom
shaped like montgolfier's first balloon
or like an amphora from ancient crete

eve's bite a shock of sweetness
and it left behind an open mouth
inviting penetration of red seeded flesh
irresistible to the first created man

and the eyes of both were opened
and they knew that they were naked
and they sewed fig leaves together
to hide their nakedness

but I can't guarantee
that if I were adam and given a second chance
I wouldn't take another juicy bite

1 October 2012

NOTES FOR RED RIDING HOOD

Little Sophie Riding-Hood
industrious girl, of family good
studying for Nursing BSc (Hons)
on placement,
Intending learning outcomes
emphasise patient-centred care, integrate theory with practice
and acquire professional competence.
50% of time on placement, gaining first hand work experience.
Live simulations bring the practical realities of the profession
directly to your studies.
Virtual Case Creator software
virtual scenarios to let you experience practicalities
of patient operations, assessment and care
SIM Men- breathing and talking mannequins
attached to monitors replicating conditions
such as falling blood pressure and cardiac arrest
real life situations which require your response

Sophie is on placement with the Community Nurse.
Her supervisor sends her on ahead
(smart in her red uniform
favoured by Southampton student nurses)
to visit an elderly service user
ill and isolated in the New Forest
Sophie knows she must not give or accept refreshment
without a prior risk assessment

The door is on the latch
come in dear
hoarse quavering voice from the darkened room
I'm so ill, can't reach
the water jug beside my bed
and I need to be toileted...

Why granny dear you look so pale
high on the Edmonton Frail Scale

grandma now I have to state
your behaviour's inappropriate
I can't administer refreshment
without a prior risk assessment

....

my insight into wolf digestion
raises an important question
crucial to the creation
of my third year dissertation

The helpless wolf went all to pieces
and howled "I'm an endangered species!"
as he saw himself become
a student nurse's learning outcome
Mr Wolf, you've had your day
You're on the Liverpool Care Pathway!

MY FREEDOM

I carry my Freedom next to my heart
on a seat reserved for the elderly
while damp oystercard holders
sway above me with envious eyes.
At Freedom's touch, steel barriers rise.
Don't take away my Freedom
with a mean means test, or tax its potency.
It doesn't expire till 2015
a guarantee I will live till then
and when I arrive at Heaven's gate
not for me the winding queue:
one touch of my Freedom and I'll go through.

November 2012

FRANK

He was a frog, a fish, a toff with a monocle
spoke with a dozen different voices
eyes black cherries full of mischief
hands like heron's wings
head a glossed aubergine
with a smile of dazzling cashews
the teeth, still his pride at ninety-five,
blazing glamour above the red carpet.

Film maker, cabaret artist,
impressario, communist,
(once an accountant in a bowler hat
until he said goodbye to that)
creative as ever a man could be
and when I was a child, so kind to me.

He was trapped in a ward they call The Oaks
the double doors unlocked, the air
turned off from sunlight to a dusty gloom;
empty atrium, curving corridor,
patients wearing other patients' rags
shuffled past identical grey doors
muttering words whose meanings they had lost.

There I found him: gazing with unseeing eyes
brain infected with spores and plaques
riddled and split in yellowing flakes
rotted and rotten, pitted and pitiful.
But then he recognised me
and sang his number about Hitler and Mussolini.

QUAND JE TE VOY
after Pierre de Ronsard, 1524-85

When I see you alone, devouring newsprint,
filigrees of wrinkles flickering round your eyes,
pouting in spasms you're not aware of;

or in your blue parka with white stuffing leaking out,
as you glide in a private world of sprouting beans,
chard and seed potatoes;

or when you involuntarily make a sound
signifying a thought you want to share
and the sun highlights a grey filament
in your miraculous brown hair;

I sometimes want to speak, but tongue and mouth
choke on a suffocating pulse of love
until I meet the radiance of your eyes
and know that what I feel, you feel for me.

Arvon, October 2013

PASTICHE

As always with the best oysters
It was like swallowing a gobbet of phlegm
From a benevolent god

"Fig" turned out not just to be a fig
roasted in vanilla butter and honey
but served with a wafer thin disc of the fruit
compressed in a sous-vide bag
to concentrate the flavour:
plus fromage frais mousse
caramelised white chocolate chunks
and figleaf ice cream.

"Cod" was actually whipped smoked roe
with deep-fried pig skin and seaweed
"Chicken" was skin again
with bacon jam and mascarpone.

Wine to drink with pork:
Chianti: take a mouthful
and roll it around on the tongue
coat your gums and feel
your mouth pucker and cluck
Take a mouthful of pork, swig again
and see how the wine invigorates the mouth, leaving you
ready for more pork. Fabulous!

Or try Tre Vescovi
Barbera can be a ruffianly kind of grape
of rustic tannins and ungainly acidity.
This however is the posh side of Barbera
with a faint prickle of fizz
cherry and damson fruit
gentle tannins and elegant length

But best of all is Verdelho
stunning lime and honeysuckle scented
from deep down under.
Its acidity carves through the rich pork
while the fruitiness picks up the pear flavours
twirls them around
and does a tasty little two-step

October 2012
*With acknowledgments to the Times
Magazine, Sunday Times "Style"Magazine
and Waitrose Kitchen*

ADDRESS TO A DEEP-FRIED MARS BAR

Upon a dark Stonehaven night
A genius took a couthie bite
In Carron's Chip Bar;
Och no! it wasna his intention
But he had made a new invention
A deep fried Mars bar!

A deep fried Mars bar hits the spot
For it will cause your teeth to rot
And make ye fatter;
Nane will resist the runkl'd pelt
Ready in his mouth to melt
Deep fried in batter!

Soft and warm and sickly-sweet
Ye bite, and caramel squirts eet
And makes a mess upon your feet-
It disna matter:
A Mars bar supper piled wi' chips
Is Heaven to your greedy lips
To swell the painch and widen hips
All on one platter!

O symbol of a nation's diet
You fuel the druken thrang this night
To brave the dangers:
Huddled wi' mufflers on their hands
Upon the tiered supporters' stands
Where Celts meet Rangers!

(wi' apologies to the Haggis)
February 2013

WALLABY AMONG THE GRAVES

A wallaby squats in Highgate Cemetery
Grazing on ivy around gravestones
Of Karl Marx, George Eliot and Jeremy Beadle.
It wanders about as bold as brass,
A non-native species,
Like the ring-necked parakeets, arachnids
And occasional muntjak deer:
A Bennett's wallaby, macropus rufogriseus.
Hailing from Tasmania.

No animals have been reported missing
From Golders Hill Park zoo.
Staff are leaving cut fruit and vegetables
For the gentle marsupial,
Friend of the Highgate Vampire
And shrouded ghosts
That lurk at twilight by Assyrian tombs.

26 October 2013

With acknowledgement to the Ham & High

BETTER TOGETHER

Auchterarder, Aberuthven, Findo Gask, Dupplin Cross,
Green Loaning, Tullybannocher, Sheriffmuir, Muckrachd,
Forteviot, Kinfauns, Auchtermuchtie, Inchyra,
Glencarse, Glendrick, Pitroddie, Battledykes,
Inchture, Abernyte, Kinnaird, Long Forgan,
Carnoustie, Trottick, Claverhouse, Mill o' Mains,
Fintry, Moatmill, Shielhall, Kellas,
Inveraldie, Murkoes, Teeling, Kirriemuir,
Nether Finlarg, Happas, Kincaldrum, Inverarity,
Kirkbuddo, Coupar Angus, Oathlaw, Bolgardo,
Finavon, Noranside, Edzell, Inchbare,
Dun, Oatyhill, Lower Scotstown, Mill of Conveth,
Auchenblae, Fordoun, Pitskelly, Drumlithie,
Glenbervie, Kinneff, Tempe of Fiddes, Barras,
Lumgair, Spurryhillock, Ecclefechan, Myrebird.

Newton Bromswold, Wetheringsett, Brundish Street, Tannington,
Wenhaston, Brabling Green, Poys Street, Peasenhall,
Pettistree, Hacheston, Mickfield, Dallinghoo,
Culpho, Bealings, Kettlebaston, Drinkstone Green,
Sicklesmere, Puttock End, Groton, Chickering,
Stowlangtoft, Little Wratting, Horringer, Thelnetham,
Charles Tye, Shimpling, Tostock, Eye,
Tuddenham, Widdington, Stow Cum Quy, Upend,
Landbeach, Waterbeach, Upward, Swavesey,
Impington, Herringswell, Witchford, Thistley Green,
Kneesworth, Horningsea, Stagden Cross, Butcher's Pasture,
Helions Bumpstead, Duck End, Ugley, Nasty,
Chithurst, Dumpford, Itchingfield, Spithurst,
No Place, Pity Me, Occold, Thrandeston,
Cratfield, Halesworth, Theberton, Covehithe.

Proud to be Scottish.
Content to be English.
Glad to be united.
Better together!

August 2014

SELF - PORTRAIT?

In childhood they told me I had big ears
And my voice was too deep:
My ears are still large but not outsize
And my voice is no deeper than yours
But the space between the ears is a mystery.
How to explain the songs I sing
Under the shower and about the house
Especially when alone:
Horst Wessel Lied, a satisfying shout
Or my song about the word Kultur
That made Goering reach for his gun:
Or a traditional lilt in minor key
About a hypocrite in a house of prayer?
Or my greed, heaping up muesli
Figs and apricots and sliced banana
Two kinds of yoghurt and semi-skimmed milk
To devour with the Times obituaries?
Why do I find it so hard, every day,
To throw anything, <u>anything</u> away?

Am I demented? The case is not closed:
I have a rapport with the diagnosed ......

April 2013

16

WE HAD THE EXPERIENCE, BUT MISSED THE MEANING

We had the experience, but missed the meaning.
We went into the Louvre and saw the Mona Lisa
and all you could think about was mending the bloody freezer
We had the experience, but missed the meaning.

We strolled along the boulevards, we clambered up
Montmartre
and all you could bring yourself to say was, Who was this
Jean-Paul Sartre?
We had the experience, but missed the meaning.

Arvon, 5.7.2012

SEARCHING QUESTIONS

What do you love?
I love a plate of Jordans muesli fresh figs apricots banana and
Rachel's gooseberry yoghurt
I love waking with you asleep on your front beside me
I love stomping round Highgate ponds talking to grebes and
Egyptian geese
I love to support people with complex problems
I love to take naps on the floor with a soft pillow

What do you hate?
I hate hoovering but I do it for you
I hate confinement in airless rooms watching slide presentations
I hate the playful condescension of my ageing dentist

What do you fear?
I fear losing you
I fear dependence
I fear incomprehension
I fear loneliness
I do not fear death

What do you want?
I want always to have ways of giving as well as receiving
I want to care as well as being cared for
I want to go on breathing the early morning air as long as I breathe
I want your next book to succeed
I want my children and grandchildren to be fulfilled
I want to express thoughts I never knew I had in poetry

Where do you live?
I live in Highgate on the edge of Hampstead Heath
our garden is crossed by foxes and feral cats
I look out onto woods and the arches of an oligarch's palace
I climb Kite Hill to see St Pauls and the Shard
I sit with you at the edge of a copse which is either
the tumulus of an ancient British warrior
a 17th century rubbish dump or both

What do you dream?
I dream of lying in a woodland grave my bones mingled with yours
I dream of my grandchildren being as happy as I have been
At night I dream constantly
and wake up forgetting the visions in my brain
I dream of reaching out for you every morning

OUR TOWN

To be sung by a male chorus wearing flat caps, holding beer glasses

Our town 'as an 'arbour
It's always full of ships:
And orf them comes a stream of dagos
Krauts an' wops an' nips:
Yids an' niggers, wogs an' chinks
And pakis come galore:
SO 'ELP US NIGEL FARRAGE*
AND DON'T LET IN NO MORE!

No more, no more! No more, no more!
So 'elp us Nigel Farrage
And don't let in no more!

Just get us aht of Europe
We never wanted in
We don't want no more regulations
Comin' from Berlin
Today it's the Rumanians
And soon we'll get Ukrainians
And vampire Transylvanians
All drinkin' blood next door....

No more, no more! No more, no more!
So 'elp us Nigel Farrage
And don't let in no more!

June 2014

* Pronounced "Farridge"

MAINE SAIL

sail down east
in milk white fog
feel your way from buoy to buoy
through bells and horns

the further east you sail
the more fog you will meet
feel your way from buoy to buoy
through bells and horns

pass Schoodic Point
Mistake Island
Moose Peak lighthouse
long finger of Petit Manan

Roque Island
no human sound
slap and slide of water
crash of waves on invisible north shore

distant buoy bells
evensong of gulls and blackbirds
clouds like dolphins
yellow light of sinking sun

moonless night
meteors fizz
satellites move and wink
among the stars

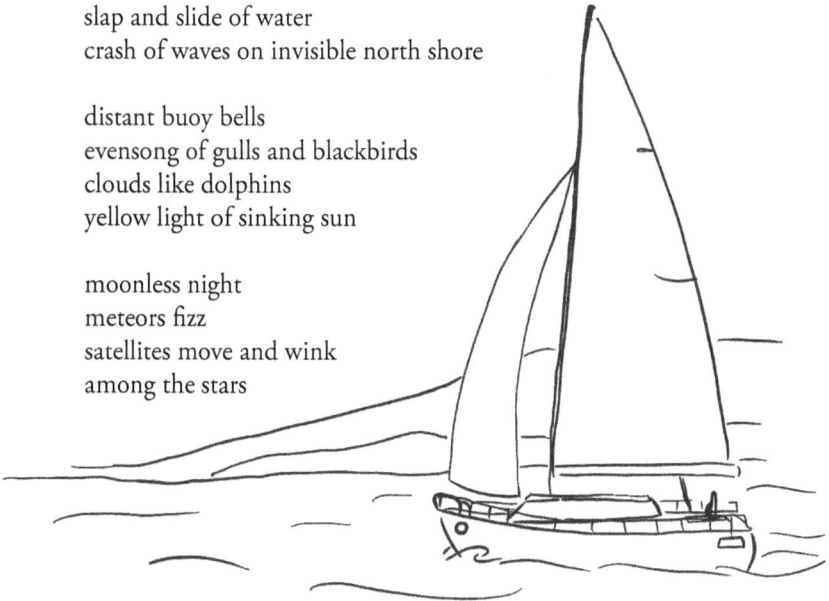

OTTO CARIUS

Iron Cross, Knight's Cross with Oak Leaves:
All the Fatherland saluted you.
Weasel faced, like a cousin of Goebbels,
in the battle group of Hyacinth Count Strachwitz
von Grosse-Zauche und Camminetz
you won your laurels in a Tiger Tank,
obliterating Soviet T-34s.
O no, you never joined the Party.

Combat troops, in your opinion,
should not be smeared with the broad brush of guilt:
so you called your pharmacy Tiger-Apotheke
wrote your memoir, Tigers in the Mud,
and your death at ninety-two
was crowned with a Times obituary.

With acknowledgment to the Times,
13 February 2015

MATING CALLS

1987 July height 5 feet attractive,
kind hearted daughter
with excellent character,
in a government Nursing School,
possesses substantial assets.
Govi Buddhist parents,
retired government officers,
seek educated, kind-hearted partner.
A son who is willing to stay in our house
is preferred. Please apply
with the horoscope.

Loyal, cuddly M, 49,
Considerate, sincere, good-hearted,
seeks f, 35-55, for good times
and r/ship. Dorset. Call me now.

Father invites marriage partner
who can give pardon for wrongdoing
for his unmarried daughter
who is a Karawa Buddhist,
33 years, pretty, having the knowledge
of English, Computer, Beauty Culture
and domestic work
and unemployed. Horoscope essential.

Seeking lady
to turn the winter of discontent
to one of content
for tall, attractive M, late 60's,
travelled, athletic, articulate,
all-round good egg.

Parents and all family members
seek a daughter who is pretty
with good character
if property is available,
and good for their son, who is close to Kandy.
Born in 1984,
respectable family,
having high income from his internet self-employment,
teatotal/non-smoker, 5 ft 4 in,
handsome and having properties.
Bank, teacher preferred, but
if unemployed, no problem.
Send details by a letter.

Wanted: loyal millionaire.
Unusual, quirky lady, 45,
used to the good things in life,
seeks attractive, mature,
exciting, stable millionaire
for r/ship. Herts. Call me now.

Just call me Mr Grey,
M, 63, tactile, kind, fun-loving,
Seeks F who finds it hard to be good.
Yorks. Call me now.

Honest, active F, 84,
retired teacher, likes reading, bridge,
keeping fit & travel.
Seeks like-minded M
for r/ship and more.
Kent. Call me now.

Honest, straightforward F, 47,
fat, fat, fat,
seeks tall, fat, fat, fat M
to share the simple things.
To the stunning redhead
who gets off at Waterloo
at about 6.30 am
wearing a grey coat and black boots
I'd love to meet you for coffee
but I'm tongue-tied.
Man with Beard and Glasses.

With acknowledgment to the
Sri Lanka Sunday Times,
the London Times and Metro

SPECIAL BIRTHDAY

"Even in his eighties
He carried on the way he did before".
Now as I approach that "even"
I baulk and turn away.
How long to disregard my breaking teeth
And fluids seeping round my ankles,
Memories flickering with delayed returns,
The barbers' harvest of grey shrivelled hair?
How long before a Camden social worker
Assesses me for person centred care
With reminiscences about the war?
Yet, when I read "He died at eight-four"
I think, a good age, a full life's span.

I dial the number of a social client
Ninety-two, bright as a diamond,
Gujurati, caring for his wife,
Surveying London from the seventeenth floor.
He knows my voice at once.
"O Michael," he says "it is so good
When you advise me;
You are an old man, and you understand."
My right side warms to hear his praise:
My left side shrivels at the breath of winter.

As life speeds up and friends drop off
The years ahead diminish their returns.
It's time to organise your legacy
Before your own worm turns;
To fashion your monument, and be
Your own stonemason

Hammers, axes, percussion hammers,
Chisels and abrasive instruments

To split, drill, grind, cut, shape and finish
A cube, a cylinder and a ball
Pediment springers and ramp and twist work
Dress stone and finish the surface
Inlay lead to lettering or shapes
Carved into stone surfaces
All to proclaim who you might have been.

I'd rather go for a woodland burial
Your bones and mine in one embrace
Like the contented imprint on our sheet.

June 2015

SPECULATION

I met the Devil on the City Road
I recognised him by his eyes that glowed
Horns concealed beneath a bowler hat
Tail in the trousers of a plutocrat.
He greeted me "Good afternoon, my friend,
Allow me to encourage you to spend:
I'll make your life enjoyable and pleasing
With the help of quantitative easing."

"With the help of quantitative easing
I'll make your life enjoyable and pleasing:
Allow me to encourage you to spend."
He greeted me, "Good afternoon, my friend."
Tail in the trousers of a plutocrat
Horns concealed beneath a bowler hat
I recognised him by his eyes that glowed
I met the Devil on the City Road.

2015

WOODLAND GRAVE

Come, with simplicity lay me out:
no screaming, sheltered from the common heat
in wide-on woodlands shadowing my thighs.
No drugs prescribed to hold me in this bed.
No eulogies around my woodland grave
But rooks that shout their calls like cheerful pigs
Brown butterflies with eyes on tattered wings
A road that murmurs in another world.

Life, your college days are over now:
My skin and flesh will slowly rot away
Feeding the trees, the worms and butterflies.
But when you join me finally one day
In one embrace we'll leave a trace behind
Like the contented imprint on our sheet.

Totleigh Barton, July 2015

MOUNT EBAL 2019*

And the social workers shall speak
And proclaim to all the service users in a loud voice:
Cursed be he who doth not deliver the vision
And the service users shall say: Amen.
Cursed be he who is not fit for purpose
And the service users shall say: Amen.
Cursed be he whose behaviour is inappropriate
And the service users shall say: Amen.
Cursed be he who is not gender neutral
And the service users shall say: Amen.
Cursed be he who maketh no SWOT analysis
And the service users shall say: Amen.
Cursed be the patriarchy
And the service users shall say: Amen.
Cursed be he who maketh no risk assessment
And the service users shall say: Amen.
Cursed be he who hath no aims and outcomes
And the service users shall say: Amen.
Cursed be he who consumeth sugar
And the service users shall say: Amen.
Cursed be he who endangereth species
And the service users shall say: Amen.
Cursed be he who useth plastic bags
And the service users shall say: Amen.
May they rise up the Edmonton Frail Scale
May they descend the Liverpool Care Pathway
May Hammond extinguish their benefits
And the service users shall say: Amen.

* See Deuteronomy 27.15

BIRD PREY

a puddle of fluff
on the old green carpet

at my feet a bird book cutout
gold and blue and beaked and black
and when I lift it up
thin and stiff as paper
delicately disembowelled
its silvery hatchet blows of song no more

the predator
crouches by the bed
watching

November/December 2015

MIDNIGHT IN LALIBELA

Abuna Yoseph, shadow mountain
under a canopy of stars

pulses of Amharic song
bounce round the hills, till muffled by a spur
only to blast again across the void

through my binoculars I see
a silver smudge,
a jewelled ball, a nest of universes:
constellations sideways, hard to recognise

February 2016
(edited at Arvon with Mimi Khalvati,
September 2016)

SNAKE PIT IN ETHIOPIA

Wukro Chirkos, Abreha Atsbeha, Selassie Begum:
it was one of those churches, hewn from rock,
temples of Solomon, baked in Gheralta sun:
dim, draped and carpeted,
jewelled with the faces of Syrian saints
and Belai Kemer, the happy cannibal,
gobbling chunks of tasty human flesh,
redeemed from the gates of Hell by Mary's mercy
for giving a beggar one drop of filthy water.

It was one of those churches: but as we turned to go
the white robed priest shouted in terror,
seized a long pole and ran outside,
stabbing and thumping the slot of an empty grave
where a snake lay, making the holy church
unclean with the misery of Adam's curse.
He thumped and stabbed, then grunted satisfaction.
The covenant of mercy was restored.

When the priest left, we turned back to see
the headless corpse St George had left behind.
Down on the grave's rock floor,
agile, supple and very, very small,
Lamprosis Fuliginosus, a brown house snake,
searched for a juicy mouse to eat for lunch.

March 2016

NIGHT JOURNEY TO SCOTLAND
JANUARY 1941

the train might get bombed
the train might get bombed
blue lights
the train might get bombed
blue lights
lavatory blocked
I'm feeling queer
the train might get bombed
the train might get bombed
the night is clear
if it goes cloudy
goes cloudy goes cloudy
they won't hear
nothing to fear
mum is here
Rhoda is here
the train might get bombed
no all clear

April 2016

FAREWELL TO HIMSELF: FEBRUARY 1989
for Martina

All Saints Kilmalooda
outpost of the Church of Ireland
stands in a rough green valley
oppressed by horizontal cloud
making twilight at midday.
In the churchyard, unfenced from the fields,
I pass an open grave, with standing spades.

Himself fell asleep in January.
The ragged protestant boy
who played barefoot in Cappoquin
(fortune and company now long gone)
will be interred today, in his best suit and tie.

Turning to enter the neo-gothic porch
I face a group of rough men,
a mute parade, heads bared in rain,
reproach to the well dressed mourners.

The Lord was his shepherd
he made and lost money
in the midst of life we are in death.
So out into the wall of icy sleet
to the waiting grave, with standing spades.

Head for the wake at Lisselan:
pepperpot tower tucked in trees,
protestant clergymen, catholic priests
and Liam Collins, Michael's cousin
revered in Clonakilty.

June 2016

SMALL VESSELS
For Mimi and Ian

Don't edit out the strange bits: own them.
Let the subject come to meet the form.
Conscious intention brings you to the door
of the poem: leave it there like a suitcase.
Walk into an unknown space, where you
discover what you think, or know, or say.
Be at your most passive to receive
sonnets that reach out to take your hand.

Breath in a poem-shaped idea
like petrichor, earth after rain:
white space around it, breathe it in:
explore and taste the goldfish.
A poem is a meteor, burns itself out.
Don't edit out the strange bits, own them!

Arvon, September 2016

THEROPITHECUS GELADA

Large stocky primate
dark brown to buff coarse pelage
dark brown face with lighter pale eyelids.
In adult males
a long, heavy cape of hair.

Short stocky fingers
and highly opposable thumbs.
Specialized dentition
for a graminivorous diet
abrasive to teeth.
Every chest displays a trademark
hairless pink hour glass.

A shuffle gait
in a sitting position:
a horde of them on the hillside
shuffle together on their bums:
a collective slowly moving crouch.

They shuffle and eat all day
but socialize at dusk,
when kids jump down on the alpha males
pulling their hair, squeaking with delight.

At night they cling to precipices
safe from predatory teeth and claws.

(with acknowledgment to
Wisconsin Primate Research Centre)
November 2016

EGYPTIAN GEESE

Sacred in ancient Egypt
they watch the dead
from walls of tombs.

Pinkish-brown overall.
Face white, dark patch around the eye,
giving a startled expression.

They breed in tree holes,
or old crow's nests,
or on the ground.

Voice harsh, honking and quacking.
They eat seeds, leaves, grasses and plant stems
and pair for life.
The male clucks quietly, like a hoarse duck:
attracts its mate
with neck-stretching and feather displays.

But if a predator appears,
the female takes command
and with a fusillade of quacks and cries
soars up to safety in the trees.

On a January morning
here they are by my feet,
grazing a tasty patch of grass,
the male muttering, the female munching,
both oblivious of me.

They munch and mutter and I drink them in
the red and black and white and grey
the ancient black ringed eyes
as they waddle and munch at my feet.

But then a honk honk HONK HONK HONK
from the female, why this consternation,
why are they taking off
to circle and gabble in the trees?

I hear another female voice:
"Bagel! Bruno!" then I see
two muddy pooches waddling at my feet,
wrapped in their winter coats against the cold:
their lady's ringlets dangling by her phone.

A glint of sun illuminates the Shard.

January 2017

PARTY POLITICS

Oxford Student Union
bans vicars and tarts parties:
offensive if one abhors
traditional gender roles.

The equalities officer
of Bristol Student Union
prohibits a chav-themed social night
appropriating working class culture
with a track suit bottom dress code.

Edinburgh Student Association
outlaws camp men,
mexicans, native americans,
gangsters, arabs, Pocohontas
and mental patients.

Newcastle Student Union
forbids publicity
flaunting gratuitous nudity
and cleavages.

With acknowledgment to The Times,
11.2.2017

DEVIL MAY CARE

Hell begins at Finsbury Park, and there
under the tangled chaos of its bridges
a tunnel leads to my retirement home.

The teeth in my three mouths have decayed:
Iscariot and Brutus have escaped
and claws now broken off, no longer slice.

Instead I take the mini-mental test.
Who is the president in Heaven?
What makes two and two? Who are these parasites

climbing down the bristles of my hair
until they reach the pivot of my thighs?
Could they be Islington social workers

assessing my needs for person centred care
or vampires who cause trouble for night staff?
Why are my thoughts immobile in the ice

scrawny like straw in glass? Now glorious evil
has shrunk to apps encrypted on my phone
dead to the touch of my arthritic claws.

My hooves removed, exchanged for slippers
so that I won't disturb the other residents
my horns sawn off and nailed outside my door

just to remind myself of who I was.

February 2017
(See Dante's Inferno, Canto 34)

PRIVATE WORLD
for Susan

Before you can remember
they gave you Teddi
to cuddle in your cot,
warming your sleep
even when his stuffing leaked
and pink faded to grey:
still comforting you in bed
when you were seventeen, in Oxford,
until I took his place.

But you kept the doll
from your fourth birthday,
your most magnificent present ever.
She came with a nightdress
and christening robe
and had real eyelids that opened
when you sat her up. She stared at you
with disapproving round green eyes,
two perfect teeth beneath her upper lip.

You named her Private Dolly
meaning that her delights were just for you
not to be shared with anybody else.

Now her cheeks are cracked
and her limbs held on by a blue jumpsuit;
mauled
by seven granddaughters.

March 2017

OTHER WORLDS

where Mochu-Pochu join
male and female rivers
Punakha Dzong
fortress of Schadrung
father of Bhutan
floats on jacaranda

an egret in the mist
gleams from Rapti's shore
as we drift towards Narangyeni
and Ganges

Bagmati
Nepal's holy river
two black draped corpses
larger than life
burn for heaven

along the village street
girls in purple smocks
skip from their first day in school

peaks of Dhaulagiri
Lantang
Manakumana and
Ganesh Himal

May 2017

THIMPU

all night
a choir of community dogs
sprawled around streets and clock tower
bark lamentation:
from birth comes decay, death,
pain, grief and despair

birth is the pivot of sorrow

from my house I still hear them:
dogs bark in the distance
craving sadness

May 2017

WHEN THE WORLD'S NOT WATCHING

I curl in a ball with a pillow and sleep on the floor
I talk to Egyptian Geese on Highgate Ponds
I drag secret chains through semolina pudding
I watch clergymen turn into rockets
I walk down tube tunnels in front of a train
I pour pea soup on invasive cats
I wander through palaces of sugar cane
I drool with delight at funeral orations
I generate imagery like an aircraft carrier
I swim in ink where seals compose
I bottle up emotions and pickle them
I abandon hope when I have entered here
I slide down the slipway into nothingness

Arvon, July 2017

CENTRE OF ATTENTION

My sister called me into her bed
and cuddled me, which she never normally did
and said "I've something to tell you."
"Has Dad died?" I asked. "Yes" she said.
My mum sat in a dressing gown,
her eyes red, worn out with crying.

I had to go to school. They were all so impressed.
When the headmaster told the children in assembly
my Dad had died, I became
the centre of attention.
When I came home, women leaned over garden walls.
"You puir wee laddie" they said.
I was enchanted

Only later I had dreams of him
stepping out of wardrobes
and vanishing into trains.

Arvon, July 2017

IN THE FOOTSTEPS OF BASHO

Following the example of John Keats, I walk down Millfield
Lane accompanied by his ghost. We admire Parliament Hill.
I sing

O snail
Climb Kite Hill
but slowly, slowly!

That is no haiku, says Keats, it has only 12 syllables. What do
you know?, I ask. He replies

I know
my heart aches
and a drowsy numbness pains my spirit.....

No, no! I rebuke him, there are no nightingales here. Only
kite flyers and tourists gaping at the Shard.

We descend, with a straggle of cross country runners, to the
dog pond. Two mandarin ducks beg for stale bread. A leaf
flutters to the water.
Season of mists and mellow fruitfulness,

Keats murmurs. Please be realistic, I tell him, this is a season
of mud and midges.

Keats stumbles over a broken bottle and gashes his leg. Yikes,
a bloody Grecian Urn, he yells, and takes flight over the trees
to Hampstead.

Arvon, July 2017

PRESS-UPS

I saw the Devil shopping in Brent Cross
I saw a pan of frying paperclips
I saw a politician in a pie
I saw an octopus on roller-skates
I saw a serpent hanging round your neck
I saw an alien in Café Rouge
I saw a tomcat lifting his long tail
I saw a poet teaching lunacy
I saw a genius biting his toenails
I saw a kettle bubble on the boil.

I saw the Devil frying paperclips
I saw a pan shopping in Brent Cross
I saw a politician on roller-skates
I saw an octopus in a pie
I saw a serpent sit in Café Rouge
I saw an alien hanging round your neck
I saw a tomcat teaching lunacy
I saw a poet lifting his long tail
I saw a genius bubble on the boil
I saw a kettle biting his toenails

Arvon, July 2017

MEMORY PROBLEMS

men who can't remember names
write copiously and then give up because
they can't remember names

men who can't remember names
see images of craving they can't feed
because they can't remember names

men who can't remember names
take flight in fantasy but feel no shame
because they can't remember names

men who can't remember names
drink coffee from familiar mugs
habit propels them through the day

men who can't remember names
see the world through half closed eyes
delusional as a game of thrones

men who can't remember names
lie in rooms with workhouse windows
watching the shadows of the nuns

men who can't remember names
drool and nod as they are fed
and moan when they are put to bed

men who can't remember names
evade the issue smile and nod
and blame their Alzheimers on God

Arvon, July 2017

DREAM GIRL

vague as a cloud but suffering
the cuts and bruises of reality
my mother was a cloud of childish hair
anxious for her siblings and her kids
devouring Dickens at the age of nine

bring down your shoes to iron she'd say
then spent the evening on the phone
to sister Sally with her stomach cold

Arvon, July 2017

HEDINGHAM CASTLE

The Norman keep looms
like a builders' lavatory
over village, woods and streams,
where a yew tree, older than the castle,
has grown for a thousand years.

We clamber down, to find
a tangle of undergrowth and bushes
dark and dank by the water.
Is this the tree,
this mess of roots and ancient broken trunks
twisting and twining round and underground?

I pick a needle, flat,
formed like a Y, poisonous to cattle,
green memento of mortality.

August 2017

MUSEUM OF CHILDHOOD

a mutton bone
with a knowing baby face
dressed in a crinoline of fabric scraps
pirouetted
from the hands of a canny kid
on the street in Bethnal Green
into the satchel of Edward Lovett
folklorist, bank clerk by day.
His collection finally took over his house
and his wife
eventually left him
but the mutton bone doll danced for me today
in the Museum of Childhood.

August 2017

HOLLOWAY ROAD- NOTES

Big Bang Chicken
Moonlight Supermarket
Cycle Surgery
Ram Books
St Mary Magdalene fitness for over-50s
Ooh-la-la
Anthea Lettings
Holloway Funeral Care
Kings Solicitors
Hair by Freda
Free Cash
Bartletts Hi-Fi
Amigos Mexican Food to Go
Malia Devi Yoga Centre
Homeburger
Haunted
Emperor Chinese Takeaway
Zia Lucia
Master Plaice
Baan Kati Thai Cuisine
North London Buddhist Centre

It's better than the Cally
Much more pally

A bald man
sits by the Nags Head
nursings his beer can like a penis

STANDARD STARTUP

built in a Pinner garage
Effie the robot
could end ironing misery

Effie dries and presses
everything from workshirts
to underwear

clothes are hung
on adjustable hangers
in an app controlled machine

for underwear
a scented ball
is added

Effie uses no more electricity
than a domestic hairdryer
a classic hardware startup

the next invention will be
an all-in-one machine
that washes dries and irons

a wife

October 2017
*With acknowledgment
to the Evening Standard 3.10.2017*

DREAM IN THE MALVERN HULLES
for Soseyn

In a winter sesoun whan softe was the sonne
we wente forth to see the Maluerne hulles.
We bifel us to slepe, for werynesse of-walked
and in a launde as we laye, lened we and slepte.
And mereylousliche, as Y may yow telle,
we saw the welthe of the world and our lyffes both.

Now Y am four score yryes and two
and thou soon four score yryes shall be:
a fair feld full of folk we have seen
and from our own loynes we have added fifteen.

October 2017

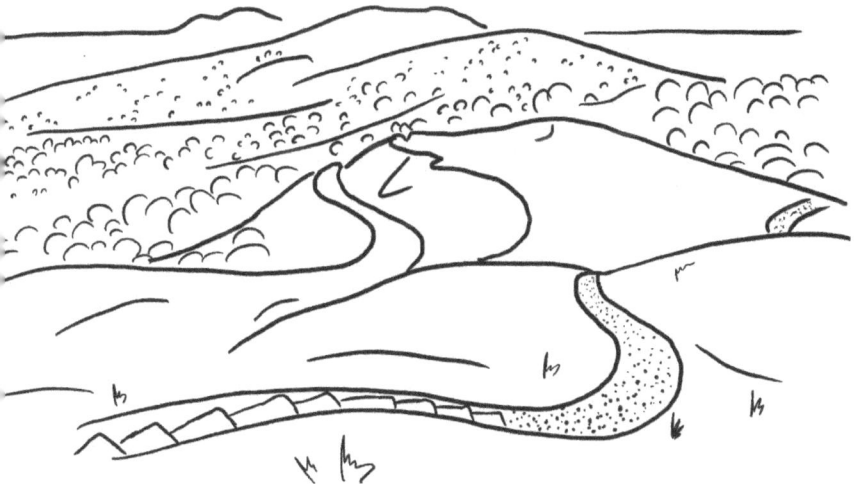

VIEWLESS WINGS

what excites me about poetry
is the gingersnap
of the hard bite
magma
that bubbles from below
on a free write

I don't want to explain poetry
but let it appear and spread on my plate
like a chocolate brownie

I'll share my brownies with others
who, like me, have a sweet tooth
for Jordan's breakfast cereal, Waitrose fresh figs
and gooseberry yoghurt

frogs may jump out of the mix and if so
good luck to them
but I won't tolerate molluscs of self analysis
or trails of slime

So Dr Freud
I don't want a diagnosis-
just to share the pleasure
of a sweet tooth

October 2017

ACCIDENT AND EMERGENCY

IF YOU NEED A CUP FOR WATER
PLEASE ASK THE STAFF
IN THE BLOOD PRESSURE ROOM
THANK YOU FOR YOUR COOPERATION

The computers are down,
all appointments are suspended
the scanner isn't charged.
Wait for the doctor
"I mean this is terrible,
Innit?"

I don't know where to go
No, not to streaming, to the toilet,
the only men's toilet is
blocked with shit and paper.
I don't know where to go,
I reported it an hour ago,
but it's still blocked.

Wait another hour for a
consulting room to come free.
When it does it will be doctor's lunchtime.

This is a basement, no daylight.
Grey as limbo, grey twisted seats,
Grey wilting patients.
Coffee and snack machines that don't work.

A door half opens and a name is called,
but not yours.

November 2017

UNCLE VILLERS

Short, gruff and bristly
he made a living selling boots
ladies' boots, all styles and fashions
from his shop in Dalston.
A paunch, his *tribuch*,
swelled beneath his waistcoat
carrying all before him.
He doted on *Seed,* his only son
who did the buying.

A widower at 69
he married auntie Beyla
whose late husband like
a wrestler in his youth
5 feet tall and 4 feet wide
broke Joe Brown's nose in Birmingham.

The deal was that
Beyla would get £5 a week and a hen
and cook the suppers Villers craved
and they would sleep in separate rooms.

November 2017

SCIENCE HAS SHOWN

101
based on a survey
of 8.3 million people
Jean Twenge
of San Diego University
finds that teens grow up more slowly
than they used to

102
eye drop makers Hycosan Fresh
have shown that women cry
4680 times in adult life
more than twice as often
as men

sad TV shows
books tiredness and rows
make the average woman cry
6 times a month
or 72 times a year

(men shed tears
only 3 times a month)

103
a survey of 8250 british adults
by National Centre for Social Research
for the supermarket Sainsbury's
found the secret of happiness
lies in a good night's sleep

104
research by Barnardos
shows that only 5% of 13 to 15 year olds
made friends at a disco
compared to 37%
of their parents' generation

105
a study by University of Reading
shows primary age kids
perform better in tests
after swallowing wild blueberry drinks
Prof Claire Williams
praised the impact of flavenoids
on the executive function of children

106
mussels clams and oysters
fart "ridiculous" amounts
of climate warming gases
scientists from Cardiff and Stockholm
have shown
equal to the methane given off
by 20000 dairy cows

107
forget the gym
doing housework
cuts the risk of early death
by a third
a global study suggests
according to data on 117000 people
in 17 countries
processed by Scott Lear
of Simon Fraser University

JEMAA EL FNA

Assembly of the Dead.

Tourists crowd
like herds of plump cows.

To flutes of snake charmers
cobras sway on concrete
lifting heads for food.

Koutoubia minaret, street food,
henna painting, acrobats,
dancers with donkey ears.

You take a picture. I feel cold contact
as coarse hands
drape two silver thread snakes
round my neck.
Cold but not slimy,
fangs removed
mouths sewn up, but leaving room
for forked tongues to protrude.

Give money, big money!
The charmer raises a fist:
twenty dirham not enough! he insists.

Cascading calls
to evening prayer
Allah-hu-akhbar
Allah-hu-akhbar, hu-akhbar, hu-akhbar
God is great
unless you're a snake
in the Assembly of the Dead.

Marrakesh, April 2018

TARBOUCHE

Like a shoebox on its side
Tarbouche opens from the souk.
Just four square tables
and a ledge round the wall
where couples perch like birds.

Through a hatch, bright light falls
on veiled heads and circling hands
creating tagines and pastillas.

Above your head
birdsong trills and thrills:
the cage is as small as a shoebox.

Stall keepers shout on Talaa Kebira
Muezzins call their flocks to evening prayer.
Come to Tarbouche
if you're feeling hungry
on a wet night in Fez.

Fez, April 2018

BLACK WATCH

Collapsed oak, dome of writhing branches,
Shattered trunk like a triceratops
On every notch and gnarl a crow
Corvus corone corone
Shouting kra-kras of triumph and reproach.

Look up to the canopy
Light
Light
They soar there
Perching on every notch and gnarl
Corvus corone corone
Shouting kra kras of triumph and reproach
Light
On their wings.

June 2018

PROMETHEUS ON-LINE

Titan Prometheus
stole fire from Zeus
and created man from clay.

Prometheus hangs upon a rock
chained to his mobile phone
while an eagle chews his liver.

When will Hercules come
to block all Olympian malware
and free the tormented Titan?

October 2018

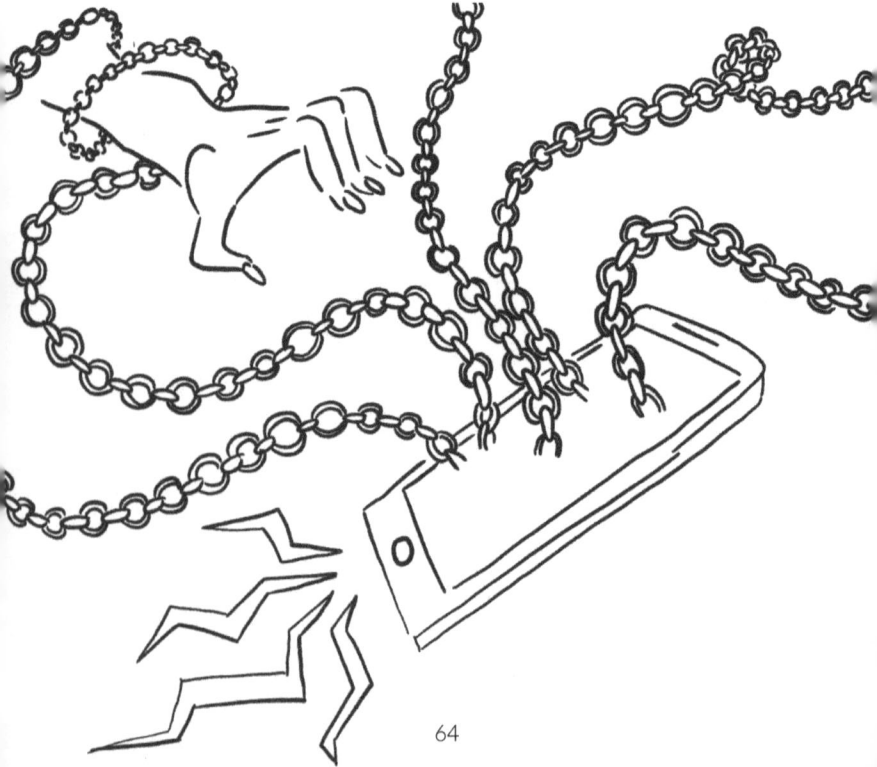

BRAVE NEW WORLD

Dance in the kitchen
to Patrick's accordion
red face contorting
red spotted handkerchief
reeking of sweat.

Dance in the kitchen
see the June stars
grey crags and misty
grey fields so sombre
Mary and Michael
are leaving, are leaving
Mary and Michael
are leaving tomorrow
are leaving tomorrow
to a New World they go
to a New World they go
a world we don't know.

Michael squeezed into
a secondhand suit
too small for his shoulders
too wide for his waist
wiping his head
on the tweed of his cap
he and his father
embracing their woe
to a New World they go
to a New World they go
to a New World they go
a world we don't know.

Mary, black haired, cheeks dimpled and red,
small mouthed, soft formed, frilled at the neck
sits with legs dangling over her bed,
loathing and longing for what is come
the love and the food and the men and the clothes
and the houses with hallways and more than three rooms
where people eat meat and ride out every day.
Soon she will leave, with her beautiful hat,
the first she has worn, and in excellent taste
to a New World they go
to a New World they go
to a New World they go
a world we don't know.

The women lament
Far over the sea
the children will go
with their hopes and their fears
and a mother's wild tears
to a New World they go
to a New World they go
to a New World they go
a world we don't know

December 2018
Inspired by Liam O' Flaherty's short story
"Going into Exile"

SMART DORMICE ON THE M1

Once a delicacy in ancient Rome
dipped in honey and poppy seeds
they are born hairless and helpless
nocturnal, omnivorous,
(fruits, berries, flowers, nuts
and insects).

In France *dormeuse*, and here the Hazel Dormouse,
they live in family groups,
thriving in brambles
and rustling through hedgerows.

In wintertime they sleep,
tails wrapped around their heads:
fattened up in summer
to feed themselves in hibernation.
If they come out before the spring
they could die from the cold.

So 13 miles of the M1
will close for 12 nights
so that trees can be gently lowered
by cranes onto lorries
parked on the carriageway
without disturbing the dormice
asleep in brambles next to the motorway
tails wrapped around their heads.

January 2019
With acknowledgment to the Times,
4 January 2019

MARYASHA

Too young to ask the Four Questions
I was amazed by the candlelight,
the silver dishes piled with fruit,
wine, matzah, sweet and bitter herbs
and egg water.

Too sleepy to eat much
I heard the songs through a haze
and was tucked in a vast feather bed
by Booba, my grandma who made all these things.

I was thrilled when they told me
Booba was Russian.
On newsreels you saw
peasant women with headscarves
chucking grenades under German tanks
and kissing tired homecoming soldiers.
Booba was like them.

Her name was Maryasha,
she too was gnarled and bent,
clad in heaps of ancient clothing,
fierce and compassionate.

She sang real Russian songs.
Her blue eyes fixed on you
would mist over as she swayed
to her resonant voice:
nikto mi nye vernye na lyubit
mikom-oo yavernya nijal
no-one loves me
no-one cares for me

She knew about Love;
she had borne nine kids
saks boys and tri girls
tri kids in four years
(Max was a handsome man
to go to bed with).

She exploded
into throaty curses as she banged about the scullery
hunting a milk saucepan.
"Sod de bloomin' ting!
or as the tomcat got under her feet
"Paskudnyak!"
Then she emerged, calm and smiling,
with a plate of milchiger borscht.

As I grew up
I liked to drop in on the way home from school.
Over tea and chunks of yeast cake
we chatted between clothes horses.
"I may be cabbage-lookin'
but I'm not green":
and wagging a finger, she advised
"Whatever you do in life
always marry de same sex"

She spent her last years
in a desolate nursing home
no garden, nothing to see or do:
memory ebbed away:
but to the last she would tell me
how she had her nine
and would sing from her treasury of songs.

March 2019

FACING THE FUTURE

DEATH: a box to enclose
collapsed time and shrunken jowls,
discarded eyes and an open mouth:
not for ME, not for ME, for HIM, for HIM
but not for YOU! YOU must outlive ME!

Not for THEM, no, our kids –
they are creative and blooming and fruitful
BUT if YOU outlive ME
then I must die....
O really, what nonsense, I stupidly cry
DEATH is closure, so please DON'T CRY.

Turn your thick head and OPEN YOUR EYES
seize the adventure to rot and decay
EAT UP your death, JUST EAT IT TODAY!
flavoured with maggots and blue-black flesh
caught in the clutch of insensate caress

and where this will take me is anyone's guess

WAKE UP, WAKE UP AND SMELL THE COFFIN!

May 2019

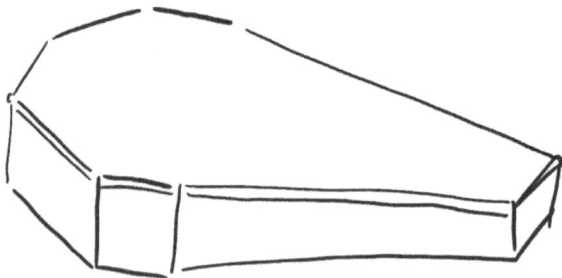

RHODA

You were my big sister
pixie-faced
just five feet when fully grown
and seven years older than me.

When hoyden Joyce came round to play
you slammed the bedroom door.
I banged in vain
and howled with indignation.

When you stood in the hall
I'd lie on the floor
to glimpse and smell your knickers.
Upskirting hadn't been invented
but I can still feel
the sting of your slap.

When I was in trouble
you stood up for me
and when you cried
I yelled at the aggressor
and when you died
twenty years ago
part of me died too

Arvon, May 2019

ARDENICA

Toiling up a stony path
we roast in midday sun
to visit Ardenica,
Albania's last monastery.

Inside its walls
the church of St Mary
has frescoes by Konstadin and Zografi
veiled in mouldy gloom.

Visit over, we pick our way
down the stony path.

Suddenly
a snake of whistle
pierces our ears,
penetrates, writhes,
twirls and tumbles.

Then we see him.
An ancient elf squats by the path side
fingering a whistle
a crumpled card beside him -
I need money for medicine and food.

In the dank church
the icons have cynical faces.
Outside, a whistle worms and writhes.

June 2019

DAWN FOX

small to medium sized omnivorous
genera of the family canidae
including kit fox arctic fox and fenner fox

digitagrad they walk on their toes
displaying drooling canines
excellent in ripping prey

most are generalist predators
but some such as the crab-eating fox
have specialist diets

foxes grip their preys neck
and shake until it is dead
or can be disembowled

at night we hear
barking yelps
and then a high pitched scream

in the morning we find him
debonair young predator
still with foxy smile

stiff and flat as a fox pancake
a wheel track visible
across his broken back

with spades we lift him up
and leave him at the kerbside
to be collected by Veolia

October 2019

LUNCH IN PARADISE

heaven behind the portals
of Lady Margaret Hall
where we kissed goodnight
sixty four years ago

seasonal forest mushroom
on sour dough toast
poached Witney egg
chives hollandaise

homemade nut & vegetable steak
on butterbean
spinach & tomato ragout
crisp parsnip
savoury red wine sauce

green apple mousse
bramley compote & apple sorbet
shortbread biscuit
Macon Villages Perelles 2017
St Joseph N Perrin 2012

heaven behind the portals
of Lady Margaret Hall
promises contentment
when we embrace tonight

October 2019

WAVES

behind Stonehaven's Board Walk
windows of bungalows
confront giant waves
wind transferring energy to water

single gigantic storm waves, building up
to fourfold the storm's wave height
and collapsing

freak waves monster waves
episodic waves extreme waves

rogue waves unpredictable
exploding on the beach
scattering foam and stones

after nightfall
in Mineral Well Park
waves of fireworks peak in tinsel plumes
burst and rattle in the rain
cheered by the soaking crowd
until the final burst
subsides into the dark

November 2019

HORN HEAD III

on ireland's northwest shore
by sheephaven
bloody foreland
falcarragh dunfanaghy
muckish mount and inishbofin
horn head splits the ocean

in bawden's painting
cows perch uneasily
drystone walls spiral
like stegosaur ribs
rocks and roofs at crazy angles

the grassy mass
sweeps upwards
obscuring the sea
blowholes
two pistols cavern
tramore beach
and mcswyne's gun

February 2020
"Horn Head III" is a watercolour by
Edward Bawden (1903-89)

ROUGH SLEEPERS

as I daydream on the northern line
staring through passengers who stare through me
a woman's voice posh like a teachers
invades our space

I have no money and nowhere to sleep
no food no help from social care
so please give generously as I come round

she circulates with practised skill
scooping donations in an old sweet tin

at first I feel resentful then I see
the torn parka and grey weary face
and drop my contribution in

outside in the rain
rough sleepers sprawl
hoods exposed in sodden sleeping bags
bedded on pavements in the smiling wind

February 2020

www.ingramcontent.com/pod-product-compliance
Lightning Source LLC
Chambersburg PA
CBHW040122070426
42448CB00043B/3479